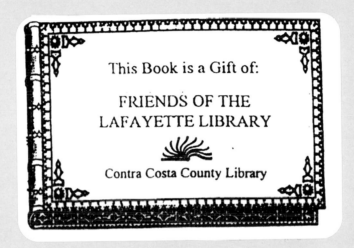

Decorated Horses

Decorated Horses

Dorothy Hinshaw Patent

Illustrated by Jeannie Brett

 Charlesbridge

Published by Charlesbridge, 85 Main Street, Watertown, MA 02472 • (617) 926-0329 • www.charlesbridge.com

Library of Congress Cataloging-in-Publication Data
Patent, Dorothy Hinshaw, author.
Decorated horses/Dorothy Hinshaw Patent; illustrated by Jeannie Brett.
pages cm
Includes bibliographical references.
ISBN 978-1-58089-362-6 (reinforced for library use)
ISBN 978-1-60734-758-3 (ebook)
ISBN 978-1-60734-643-2 (ebook pdf)
1. Horses—Juvenile literature. 2. Horses—History—Juvenile literature.
I. Brett, Jeannie, illustrator. II. Title.
SF302.P372 2015
636.1009—dc23   2013049021

Printed in China
(hc) 10 9 8 7 6 5 4 3 2 1

Illustrations done in watercolor with gouache, pastel, and colored pencil on 300-lb Arches hot-press paper
Display type set in HVD Comic Serif Pro, designed by Hannes von Döhren
Text type set in Palatino Sans designed by Hermann Zapf and Akira Kobayashi for Linotype
Color separations by KHL Chroma Graphics, Singapore
Printed by C & C Offset Printing Co. Ltd. in Shenzhen, Guangdong, China
Production supervision by Brian G. Walker
Designed by Susan Mallory Sherman

To horse-loving children everywhere—D. H. P.
For Bailey Boy—J. B.

Introduction

EVER since humans domesticated horses more than nine thousand years ago, these amazing animals have been favorite companions. Like people, horses live in family groups, so they bond emotionally to other horses—and to humans. Their intelligence and ability to relate to people make them highly trainable, allowing humans to ride them. Their strength enables them to pull heavily loaded carts and wagons.

Over the years and across cultures, horses have helped people travel, find food, conquer new lands, and defend their homes. They have brought people honor by winning skill-based competitions and have helped people celebrate special occasions. In return humans have expressed love and respect for their hardworking friends by proudly equipping and decorating them for their many roles.

Warfare and Hunting

ONCE people learned to ride on horseback, hunters and soldiers became much more effective than they had been on foot. A swift horse carrying a hunter could easily pursue large, speedy animals such as deer and buffalo. Warriors on horseback could attack and retreat much faster than foot soldiers could, and their height atop their mounts added power to the thrust of their weapons.

The earliest use of horses in war and hunting was for pulling chariots, a practice that began in ancient times in the Middle East. Horses also assisted medieval knights in Europe, carried Japanese samurai and the Mongol army into battle, and helped change the course of American history.

Chariot Horses
Swift and Fierce

A foot soldier in the Middle Eastern kingdom of Assyria waits with his comrades, spear in hand, to confront his enemy on the plains. It is 1800 BCE. A dust cloud appears on the horizon, then chariots drawn by wildly galloping horses thunder down upon him. An enemy soldier on horseback stabs downward from his high perch, and the foot soldier collapses. One of his comrades cries out as he is trampled by horses.

With their impressive battle skills, chariot armies conquered much of the ancient world, and this type of fighting was adopted by many cultures. Egyptians had mastered the art of chariot warfare and hunting by 1500 BCE. Ancient Egyptian art depicts images of one-person chariots drawn by horses wearing beautiful blankets and elaborate headdresses. The warriors wanted to make a big impression on their enemies and perhaps used the tall headdresses to make the horses look especially large and frightening.

Because chariots were so valuable for both hunting and war, they continued to spread to other cultures, reaching China by 1200 BCE.

Horses in Armor
Medieval Knights in Battle

An oldest son watches his younger brothers practice their horse-riding skills in the fields of his father's estate in Europe during the Middle Ages. He will inherit everything, leaving them landless. But all is not lost for the younger brothers—they can still gain honor and property by winning battles for the king as knights on horseback.

When knights jousted to practice and demonstrate their battle skills, their horses wore special decorative costumes and protective gear called barding. It included heavy tapestry cloths called caparisons, decorated with designs and emblems such as the knight's family crest. But when it was time for battle, both knights and their special war horses, called destriers or chargers, wore metal armor to protect them from enemy weapons. Knights on horseback often created havoc among enemy ranks as they plowed swiftly through armies of foot soldiers.

Japanese Horses
Samurai Mounts

A short, stocky horse with a bright red breast-collar and crupper shows its restless spirit by pawing at the ground. It snorts, shaking rows of graceful red fringe. The rider, a Japanese warrior called a samurai, holds the horse steady as he prepares to depart for battle.

For hundreds of years, ending in the late nineteenth century, samurai fought battles and meted out justice in Japan, spending much of their time on horseback. Most samurai protected large families, called clans, or served local rulers. The most exalted samurai served the emperor.

Japanese art depicts the beautiful red trappings that the samurai's horses wore. In Japanese culture, red is a color representing energy and power, qualities valued in a warrior. Some outfits had small decorative metal ornaments. The wide, cloth reins were often banded in blue and white, colors representing loyalty and purity.

Mongol Horses
The Greatest Mounted Army

A sound like distant thunder fills the air, growing stronger as the villagers scramble for safety. They've been warned about strange invaders dressed in leather hoods and body armor, riding armored horses. The Mongol army is approaching.

During the early 1200s the Mongols, led by the legendary leader Genghis Khan, galloped on the backs of their small, swift horses across Asia and into Europe, conquering everything in their path. The warriors' saddles, made of wood and leather, had stirrups to steady the rider as he shot arrows at the enemy. At its height the Mongol Empire stretched from Korea and modern Vietnam to Hungary, Russia, and Syria.

The Mongol army's victories would not have been possible without their tough and sturdy mounts. Mounted soldiers could gallop into settled villages to fight and could retreat quickly. Their horses carried food and cooking pots, making the soldiers mobile and therefore difficult to find.

Painted Horses

Transforming American Indian Lives

As the sun sets on the plains, a nineteenth-century American Indian warrior heads back to his people on a horse painted with symbols of shining suns, arrowheads, and other designs. The markings, which vary from tribe to tribe, record the horse's life story and are believed to increase the horse's power and protect it from harm.

Red circles around the horse's eyes were thought to give the horse keen eyesight. Arrowheads on hooves provided speed. Arrowheads painted in a line brought victory in battle. Painted zigzags gave the horse the awesome power of lightning, and painted dots meant hail would be unleashed upon an enemy. Plains Indian hunters sometimes painted their horses when they hunted buffalo, an important source of food, clothing, and material for making tools.

American Indians didn't always have horses. Spanish explorers brought the animals to the Americas in the 1500s, and some of the horses escaped onto the prairies. Once they had horses, many American Indians developed into superb mounted warriors. Generals in the US Army attempted to keep horses from the Indians because the Indians had become such effective mounted fighters, among other reasons.

Horses still bring pride to Plains Indians today, who use them to compete in rodeos and at powwows. Plains Indian teenagers show their courage and strength through races and endurance rides.

Performance and Competition

PEOPLE love to be entertained by performances of skill and talent, and the thrill of competition adds to the fun. Horses are natural performers and competitors. They can be trained to wear many different types of equipment and decoration, as well as to learn new behaviors and routines. They have executed synchronized routines in Tang dynasty China, competed as draft horses in North America, entertained crowds at circuses, run in historic and high-stakes races, and danced at weddings in Egypt.

Ancient China

The Emperor's Dancing Horses

One hundred horses toss their mane, braided with pearls and jade, and swish their tail, rearing up in perfect unison. Four bands of young men dressed in bright yellow shirts and jade-studded belts play a special song called "Music of the Upturned Cup." The horses climb to the top of a three-tiered platform and turn and twirl on high. Then each horse grasps a wine cup in its teeth. As the music grows to a climax, the horses raise their head to mimic drinking the wine, then wobble their head and collapse as if they were drunk. The crowd gathered in the capital city of Chang'an in eighth-century China roars in appreciation.

This ancient performance was done as part of the elaborate "Thousand-Autumn Festival" celebration held to honor Emperor Xuanzong's birthday. The event included creatures such as elephants and rhinoceroses, and acrobats and jugglers performed. But the highlight of the festivities was the emperor's dancing horses, with their delicately embroidered silken scarves, bridles of silver and gold, and entertaining performance.

Draft Horses

Gentle Giants Show Off

The air fills with the sound of jingling metal as six perfectly matched gray Percheron draft horses decked out in shiny black leather harnesses enter the ring. Each braided mane is carefully divided into spiky puffs decorated with red ribbons. The horses pull a bright red wagon driven by a man wearing an old-fashioned outfit and a black hat.

Draft horse competitions happen across the United States and Canada. The competitions are based on the work these animals were originally bred for: before engines were invented, draft horses provided power for work. Some galloped through the streets pulling fire wagons, while others quietly dragged plows through the springtime earth on remote homesteads. Some farmers still use them for work, but most draft horses today are competitors—carefully groomed and dressed for shows. Draft horses are nicknamed "gentle giants," because they are generally peaceful, cooperative animals.

Not all show-quality draft horses compete. The Budweiser Clydesdales perform around the country. Each of these huge horses stands six feet tall at the shoulder and weighs around a ton. These beautiful teams evoke bygone days when working horses were a part of everyday life.

Circus Performers

Liberty Horses Steal the Show

An elegantly dressed woman strides confidently into the show ring of Circus Krone in Germany. The crowd hushes in anticipation. The woman calls out, and eight gleaming black stallions dressed in silver harnesses and sporting puffy white plumes on their head and withers enter and trot effortlessly around the ring. They look as though they are floating. They weave back and forth gracefully and rear up in unison, with their front hooves tucked tightly to their body and their neck gracefully arched. The crowd is awed as a single command from the woman makes the horses turn as a group and move in the other direction.

Liberty horses respond to commands flawlessly, without having any physical connection to their trainers and without bearing riders—they perform "at liberty." It can take years of intensive training to produce one performance. The movements of the horses, called dressage, are based on natural movements but are refined and balanced through training. Each horse is trained alone at first, then gradually incorporated into the larger group.

Many breeds become liberty horses. Arabians are favored for their beauty and intelligence, but other breeds, such as purebred Dutch Friesians and South American Criollos, have also performed in successful and popular liberty acts.

Thoroughbred Racers
Running for Roses

It's the first Saturday of May in 1987—time for the Kentucky Derby! As the horses stride toward the gate, a commentator notes that one of the horses, Alysheba, has made a career out of coming in second or third. A bad start puts Alysheba near the back of the pack, and he stumbles. But then he rallies, using spirit and courage to surge in front of his rival, Bet Twice. Alysheba wins the derby in one of its most exciting finishes ever.

The tradition of honoring the Kentucky Derby winner with roses began more than a hundred years ago, and soon the derby became known as "the Run for the Roses." Since 1932, a large, beautiful garland of red roses has been draped over the winner's shoulders as people cheer and cameras flash. More than four hundred roses are hand-sewn onto green satin, with the seal of the state of Kentucky at one end and a number designating how many times the derby has been run at the other. One special rose stands above the rest, representing the heart and determination it takes for the winner to triumph over his opponents.

As part of a tradition starting in 1996, the garland is freeze-dried to preserve it for the horse's owner. Some owners have had one rose dipped in silver to create a permanent symbol of their champion's great victory.

Arabian Beauties

Dancing Horses of the Desert

Rhythmic drum and flute music begins, and the guests at a wedding in Egypt look up to see an elegant Arabian horse enter the room. The rider wears a simple outfit—the horse is the real star of the show. It wears a shiny, hand-decorated silver saddle. A shiny silver medallion dangles between its eyes, hanging from a silver bridle. As the horse prances elegantly in place, a decorated breastplate jingles in time to the music. The guests rock back and forth as they watch and listen.

The history of the dancing horses of the desert began hundreds of years ago, when bedouin armies fought on horseback. They faced one another, their weapons ready and their horses primed for action. As musicians beat on drums and played flutes, each eager horse arched its powerful neck and shook its head as it swayed from side to side. The horses seemed to be saying, "We are ready for battle!"

Bedouins no longer challenge each other to battle on horseback, but their horses still dance for peaceful entertainment. Seeing a performance today is a great honor and special treat.

Ceremony and Celebration

PEOPLE mark important life events and honor special days with ceremonies and celebrations. The important roles horses have played in human cultures have been reflected in events over time. Horses have been buried alongside warriors in Central Asia, pulled carts in parades in Italy, performed for traditional leaders in Nigeria, and led parades in the United States.

Scythian Horses

A Mystery Buried in Time

Fierce wandering warriors called Scythians gallop across the vast grasslands in Central Asia 2,700 years ago. They are headed to a funeral. Horses are so important to the Scythians that they are needed in the afterlife as well—a horse will be killed and buried with the dead man.

During the twentieth century archaeologists found giant burial mounds, called kurgans, high in the mountains where Russia, Mongolia, China, and Kazakhstan come together today. The kurgans had been preserved in ice for more than two thousand years. They contained the mummified remains of horses and people, as well as precious gold objects decorated with images of deer, wild boars, camels, and horses.

Some of the mummified horses wore elaborate outfits, including masks with giant wooden deer antlers covered with felt, or ibex antlers overlaid in gilt. Some had bridles decorated with graceful curlicues. Saddles sat atop beautifully decorated blankets, while the saddle covers featured bits of brilliant gold foil. Some of the textiles were made hundreds of miles away from where they were found.

Archaeologists don't know whether the decorations found in the kurgans were designed specifically for the grave or were worn for other special ceremonies. Because Scythians had no written language, details about their lives remain a mystery.

Italian Parade

Cart Horses of Old Sicily

Crowds gather along the street for a parade. Cheerful accordion music fills the air, accented by the sound of tambourines. The clip-clop of hoofbeats echoes down the streets of the village as a parade of brightly painted two-wheel carts, drawn by heavily decorated horses, passes by. It's a saint's day in Sicily.

Such carts were once used in everyday life on this large island at the southern end of Italy. Donkeys pulled them in the rocky, mountainous interior, and horses did the job on the plains and in cities. The carts, with their giant wheels and high clearance, could overcome rugged obstacles.

Today the horses that pull the carts are so heavily decorated that it can be hard to see the horse. Sometimes a huge plume sprouts up from the animal's back and another from its head. The horse is usually clothed in intricately decorated fabrics and tassels.

Each province of Sicily has its own style of decoration. Some decorations feature stories from the past, such as crusader knights fighting Arabs, while others show playful subjects like mermaids and flowers. Like the horses, every inch of the carts and wheels is covered by brightly colored designs.

West African Mounts

A Historical Drama

Twice a year huge crowds of people line the streets of Kano, Nigeria, to watch hundreds of colorful horses and riders parade by as part of a celebration called the Durbar. Sunlight flashes off intricately decorated silver bridles, neck pieces, and saddle blankets as each group of turbaned horsemen passes.

The emir of Kano sits under a large purple umbrella at the parade ground in front of his palace. He is surrounded by bodyguards. The decorated men and horses have come to pay their respects on this holiday. After parading through town to the palace, each group gallops full tilt toward the seated emir. The riders pull on the reins at the last second and raise their swords, which shine in the sun, in a show of loyalty.

Until the twentieth century, the emir ruled the surrounding region. In those days every town and district was required to provide armed horsemen to protect the emir's land in case of war. Today an elected governor holds political power, and the emir is a symbolic and religious leader.

The distinctive costumes of the men and horses indicate their region of origin. Only princes who can trace their bloodlines to the emir of Kano wear a pair of horns jutting up from their turban.

Golden Palominos

Everyone Loves a Parade!

It's time for the famous Rose Parade in Pasadena, California, and the crowd is waiting in anticipation. This year the Long Beach Mounted Police are leading the parade. Their golden palomino horses shine in the sun, and the silver on their black leather saddles flashes brilliantly. Each rider wears a bright red, white, and blue outfit, a holster with a western six-shooter, and a white cowboy hat. Each carries an American flag that flaps in the breeze.

Since 1935, local citizens have applied to be part of the Long Beach Mounted Police to honor the ranching and outdoor traditions of California. Each rider owns her or his own horse, saddle, bridle, and other tack. The group has ridden in parades all over the United States, Mexico, and Canada, and they've participated in two presidential inaugural parades.

Over time the golden palomino horse has become a symbol of the Old West and a popular parade horse for rodeo queens and other celebrities. Wherever the Long Beach Mounted Police are riding, they make a point to talk with the public about the important role of horses in California and beyond. The horses look regal with their western-inspired saddles and decorations.

Conclusion

WHETHER for warfare, performance, ceremony, or just plain showing off, people can't seem to resist the temptation to decorate horses, highlighting the beauty and spirit of these regal creatures. The decorated horse is a symbol of the respect, admiration, and affection that humans have felt for their equine companions over centuries and across the world.

Parts of a Horse

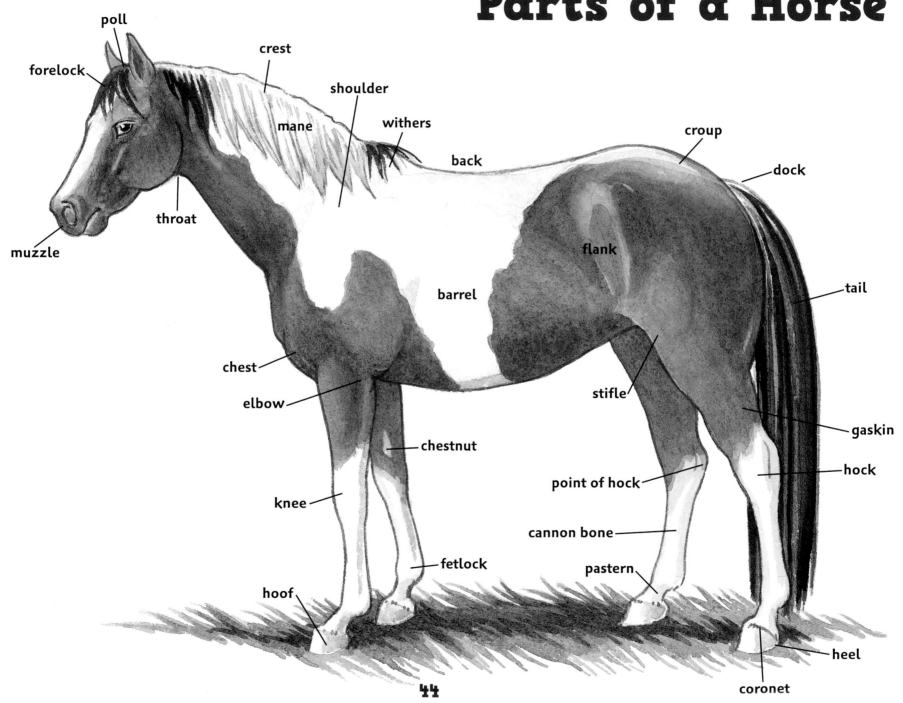

poll

crest

forelock

shoulder

mane

withers

throat

back

croup

dock

muzzle

flank

tail

barrel

chest

stifle

elbow

gaskin

chestnut

hock

point of hock

knee

cannon bone

pastern

fetlock

hoof

heel

coronet

44

Horse Tack

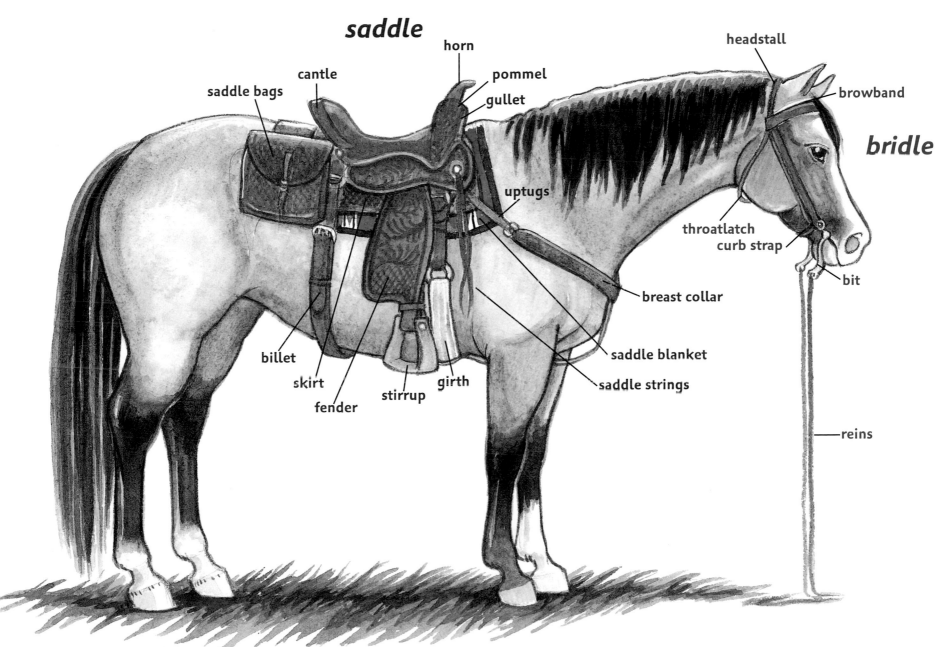

saddle

horn

cantle

pommel

saddle bags

gullet

headstall

browband

bridle

uptugs

throatlatch
curb strap

breast collar

bit

billet

saddle blanket

skirt

saddle strings

girth

fender

stirrup

reins

Bibliography

Articles and Books

Chamberlin, J. Edward. *Horse: How the Horse Has Shaped Civilizations*. New York: BlueBridge, 2006.

Chenevix Trench, Charles. *A History of Horsemanship: The Story of Man's Ways and Means of Riding Horses From Ancient Times to Present*. New York: Doubleday, 1970.

Cowdrey, Mike, Ned Martin, and Jody Martin. *American Indian Horse Masks*. Nicasio, CA: Hawk Hill Press, 2006.

Edwards, Gladys Brown. *The Arabian: War Horse to Show Horse*. Covina, CA: Rich Publishing, 1973.

Rossabi, Morris. "All the Khan's Horses" in *Natural History*, October 1994. http://afe.easia.columbia.edu/mongols/conquests/khans_horses.pdf.

Seth-Smith, Michael. *The Horse in Art and History*. New York: Smithmark, 1978.

Waley, Arthur. *The Real Tripitaka and Other Pieces*. Rockville, MD: Silk Pagoda, 2012. First published 1952 by Allen and Unwin.

Websites

Dancing Arabian horses
http://www.arabianhorses.org/education/education_history_bedouin.asp

Kano Durbar
http://www.economist.com/node/12436189

Liberty horses and circuses
http://www.ringling.com/ContentPage.aspx?id=45753&section=45696

Scythian horses
http://www.pbs.org/wgbh/nova/transcripts/2517siberian.html

Sicilian horse carts
http://www.bestofsicily.com/carts.htm

Read More

Crisp, Marty. *Everything Horse: What Kids Really Want to Know About Horses*. Minnetonka, MN: NorthWord Books for Young Readers, 2005.

Henry, Marguerite. *Album of Horses*. New York: Aladdin, 1993.

Wilsdon, Christina. *For Horse-Crazy Girls Only: Everything You Want to Know About Horses*. New York: Feiwel & Friends, 2010.

Learn More Online

Arabian dancing horses
https://www.youtube.com/watch?v=_-pS8xpMLoY

Chariot armies
https://suite.io/robert-mcroberts/59g42z5

Chinese dancing horses
http://www.chinaculture.org/gb/en_curiosity/2003-09/24/content_27769.htm

Draft horses
http://www.youtube.com/watch?v=6D34Q5icoHI
http://en.wikipedia.org/wiki/Budweiser_Clydesdales

Horses and humans
http://www.amnh.org/exhibitions/past-exhibitions/horse

Kano Durbar
https://www.youtube.com/watch?v=hl2lx9PiEwE

Kentucky Derby
http://www.kentuckyderby.com/history/year/1987
http://horseracing.about.com/od/kentuckyderby/a/aaderbyrose.htm

Liberty horses
http://www.ringling.com/ContentPage.aspx?id=45753&section=45696
http://www.youtube.com/watch?v=LZz26cx_vG0

Medieval knights and horses
http://www.horsemanmagazine.com/2009/08/war-horses-and-medieval-knights/

Painted horses
http://www.warpaths2peacepipes.com/native-american-culture/horse-war-paint.htm
http://www.texasindians.com/horse.htm

Parade horses
http://www.longbeachmountedpolice.com/horses.htm
http://en.wikipedia.org/wiki/Parade_horse

Samurai and Mongol armies
http://en.wikipedia.org/wiki/Horses_in_East_Asian_warfare

Scythian horses
http://archive.archaeology.org/0205/abstracts/scythian.html
http://www.ancientworlds.net/aw/Article/729288

Sicilian horse carts
http://en.wikipedia.org/wiki/Sicilian_cart
http://www.youtube.com/watch?v=4Qr5CTF3uks

Index